# WASHINGTON

# A Heroic Drama of the Revolution

## IN FIVE ACTS

### BY

### INGERSOLL LOCKWOOD.

Published by Left of Brain Books

Copyright © 2021 Left of Brain Books

ISBN 978-1-396-32122-1

*First Edition*

All rights reserved. No part of this publication may be reproduced, distributed, or transmitted in any form or by any means, including photocopying, recording, or other electronic or mechanical methods, without the prior written permission of the publisher, except in the case of brief quotations embodied in critical reviews and certain other noncommercial uses permitted by copyright law. Left of Brain Books is a division of Left of Brain Onboarding Pty Ltd.

# Table of Contents

CHARACTERS.

1775. ACT FIRST.

   MOUNT VERNON — A RECEPTION ROOM.

1778. ACT SECOND.

   Valley Forge—Camp-scene in Winter—Daybreak—Sentinels posted in front—Snow Storm.

1780. ACT THREE.

   BEVERLY MANOR HOUSE, WEST POINT.

1780. ACT FOURTH.

   WASHINGTON'S HEADQUARTERS AT TAPPAN--QUAINT OLD ROOM. SENTINEL VISIBLE THROUGH THE WINDOW—A STORM IN PROGRESS.

1783. ACT FIFTH.

   FRANCIS TAVERN NEW YORK.

# CHARACTERS.

George Washington, Commander-in-Chief of the American Armies.

Henry Knox,

Nathl. Greene,

Marquis De La Fayette,  } his generals

Baron Steuben, and

Benedict Arnold

Alex. Hamilton, Colonel and Aid-de-Camp.

James Caldwell, the "Fighting Parson."

Mary Washington, Mother of George.

Martha Washington, Wife of George.

Margaret Arnold, Wife of Benedict.

Janet, her attendant.

William, Washington's body-servant.

Chris,
Cad,
Moll,
Lottie,  } Slaves on Washington's estate.

An Old Soldier.

A Country Maiden.

Soldiers, Body-guard, Slaves, Attendants, Chorus of Children, etc.

## 1775.

---

## ACT FIRST.

### MOUNT VERNON —A RECEPTION-ROOM.

### SCENE FIRST.

CHRIS. — Now look aheah, you wimmin folks jis clar out an mind you bizness; go way dar, I tell ye, go way, don' ye heah? Shoo fly!

CAD. — Shan't do it, you jis better git about yer own bizness.

MOLL. —Don' ye suspec' dat us wimmin folks want to see Massa Washington all dressed up in his unicorn an appleletters, hey, you man Chris? You shoo fly, yourself!

CHRIS. — Ya, ya! Massa Washington! jes heah dat she darkey talk? Why woman, haint you got no common sense under dat wool ob yourn no how? Massa Washington! Massa Washington! Ya, ya! I'se shamed ob you. Go 'way! Go peel dose taters. Massa Washington! Why didn't Massa Washington go up to Philumadelphy and been got done made a gin 'ral ob de armies ob de whole kentry all de people ob de armies an' an' all de gemmen ob ole Virginny?

LOT. —Look aheah, you man, Chris; you jis shut up dat fly-trap ob yourn an' go finish you scrubbin'; d'ye heah me, sah? You got too much brains for one darkey's head altogedder, sah, altogedder, I say.

OTHERS. —Ya, ya, ya.

LOT. —You jes answer me dis crestion.

CHRIS. All right, gal; discharge your blunderbuss; I'll gib you all de inflamation you want.

LOT. —Is Massa Washington goin' to fight 'ginst de king?

CHRIS. —In course he is, you she lunatic; and he is goin' to gib him de biggest shakin' up he's had since he was a born chile!

OTHERS. —Ya, ya, ya!

LOT. —Well, did de king 'pint massa Washington a gin'ral?

CHRIS. -Ya, ya; why no; you done gone crazy fo' shuah!

LOT. —Well, den, who did 'pint him gin'ral?

CHRIS. —Who, who, you escaped lunatic asylum, you what's de crestion? who did 'pint him?

OTHERS. — Yes, darky who, who?

CHRIS. —Why, why, de —de—

OTHERS. —Ya, ya, dat's de crestion gib us yer inflamation, darky?

CHRIS. —Why, de members ob de —de —

OTHERS. —Ya, ya dat's zackly de crestion.

LOT. —Look aheah, darkey, you go finish dat scrubbin'.

CAD. —Whar's dat inflamation, chile? Who made Massa Washington gin'ral? dat's the crestion to be dissolved, ya ya!

CHRIS. (*Taking off his hat and looking up.*) —'Fore God, gals, I belieb someone up dar did it.

CAD. (*at the door*). —Hark! heah come Massa Washington fo' shuah.

CHRIS. —Call him Gin'ral Washington, you crazy lunatic; stan' back from dat do, let me come fast; now, gals, when he open de do' ebery one ob you call him Gin'ral Washington.

*Door opens,* WILLIAM, *in uniform, walks in pompously.*

## SCENE SECOND.

OTHERS —Ya, ya, ya!

WM. — Look aheah, what you darkies loafin' aroun' dis do' fo', hey? Moll, you go peel your taters an' Chris. Go finish dat scrubbin' you lef dat scrub-brush right in my way, mos' spile de polish on my shoe.

CHRIS — Say, Bill, chile, whar's de gin'ral, hey?

WM. —Look, aheah, darky, who you call Bill? I isn't Bill any mo', I'se William, de gin'ral's milumtary servant. Call me William, else don' ye speak to me, d'ye heah!

OTHERS. — Ya, ya, ya!

CHRIS. —Well, William, de gin'ral' s milumtary servant, whar am de gin'ral, tell us dat, chile; dat's what's de matte wid us.

WM. —Go way wid yer foolin', de gin 'ral is gibbin his distractions to de oberseer; me an' de gin 'ral we leab fo' de not right away don' ye see I'se all ready to' the journey, so now go finish dat scrubbin' an' take dat pail an' scrub' —brush out of de hall-way, don' ye heah me chile?

CAD — Ya, ya; look aheah, youngster, you're too big for dose close ob yourn, you was, for shuah you better let dat coat out behind or dere'll be disruption for shuah.

CHRIS. —Take car dere, boy tenshin, company; sojer arms; ya,ya ya! Say, gals, don't ye tink I'd make a good sojer, hey?

WM. — Go finish dat scrubbin'.

OTHERS. —Ya, ya, ya!

CHRIS —Oh, Bill —'scuse me, sah, William, de gin'ral's milumtary servant, when will de gin'ral be down? we want to see him all in his —his unicorn and appleletters.

WM. Ya, ya!

CHRIS. We want to say good mornin', Massa Gin'ral Washington.

WM. —Ya, ya, darkey, you clean gone crazy, fo' shuah. Don' ye know what de gin 'ral will say to you?

CHRIS. No, I don't, Bill, for shuah; hope to die if I do.

WM. —Why, he'll say, Chris, go finish dat scrubbin'.

OTHERS. —Ya, ya, ya!

CAD. (*at window*). — Look aheah, gals; jis look aheah, quick; see dose sojer men on horseback comin' up de lane, all in their unicorns; see deir knives hangin' by deir sides.

CHRIS. — Knives! Ya, ya! Go way, gal; dem is deir swords.

MOLL. —Heah dey come lickety split, four ob dem. Ya, ya! Harrah fo' oldy Virginny an' all de rest ob de people.

WM. —Clar out dere, you darkies; dem is de odder gin'rals what's goin' to 'scort me and Gin'ral Washington up norf to shake up dose British boys. Clar out dar, I say. Take away dat broom, Moll. Hurry up dar, Chris; pick up dat scrubbin-brush. Shoo, 'way wid you, ebbery one ob you.

CHRIS. —I say, Bill, don' you tink I'd better call de gin'ral

WM. — Clar out, chile; what's de matter? Done gone crazy to shuah. I'll call de gin'ral mysef after I receib the gemmin.

[Servants go.]

Enter KNOX and GREENE, with their aids.

## SCENE THIRD.

WM. —Dis way, gemmen; walk right in heah, if you please dis way. I'se de gin'ral's milumtary servant. My name is William, gemmen.

GREENE. —We are not too late, are we? The general has not left for the north, I hope.

WM. — Will de gemmen be pleased to 'proach de side board for a little 'freshment?

KNOX. —What, has the general left Mount Vernon? Why, they told us at Alexandria that he had not passed through there.

WM. —Will de gemmen please 'proach de side-board. De gen'ral has some werry fine cider, bottled it himself, gemmen dat is to say, me and de gin'ral bottled dat cider. Step dis way, gemmen, werry fine, to' shuah!

GREENE. — No, no, my good fellow, we've no time. If the general has set out for the North, we must follow him at once.

WM. —Beg you' pardon, gemmen, you've plenty ob time to drink a glass ob de gin'ral's cider we don't leab to' de norf fo' one hour yet.

KNOX. — Ha, ha! this fellow is good. His brass buttons have turned his head.

GREENE — Then the general is still here?

WM. — Well, no sah, not zackly heah, sah he's werry tickerly engaged, sah, gibbin his distractions to de ober seer.

KNOX. —We are in time then, gentlemen. Say to him that General Greene and Gen. Knox have arrived, and await his pleasure.

WM. —Sorry, sah can't do it, gemmen, no how. De gin'ral gib me werry tickler orders not to starb him.

GREENE. —There'll be no harm done, my good man; the general expects us.

WM. — Sorry, gemmen, but my orders, sah, are not to protrude upon de gin'ral under no skircumstances, no how. [*A bell rings, he darts out of the room.*]

KNOX —Ha, ha, ha! This fellow's brass buttons will be the death of him. Did you notice how he strutted about?

GREENE —He's the general's military servant, no doubt. He'll wear his uniform more gracefully after a few months' service.

KNOX —I hope we shall not be delayed, general —the morning is cool, we can put thirty miles behind us at a single stretch.

GREENE. — No, no, not a third of it we must spare our horses, for we've a long journey before us.

KNOX. — True, general, but in these soul-stirring times it is a difficult matter to restrain one's ardor. Would that we were in sight of brave old Boston this very moment!

GREENE. —Ha, ha, ha! But hark, I hear footsteps coming this way.

WILLIAM *throws open the door.*

Knox. — Yes, it's the general.

*Enter* WASHINGTON. (*They salute.*)

## SCENE FOURTH.

GEN. WASH —My dear generals, here's welcome, welcome to Mount Vernon! (*To the aids.*) — Your servant, gentlemen.

GREENE. —We wish you health and happiness, general.

KNOX. —And a bright and glorious career.

GEN. WASH —I thank you, my friends; I thank you from my heart. I am about to undertake a mighty task and can only cry! Heaven speed the right! But, tell me gentlemen, what news do you bring from the north? [*Motions to seats.*]

GREENE. —Oh. Stirring news, general, stirring news! The few red stains of Lexington and Concord have been washed from our remembrance by a deluge of the dearest patriot blood, shed in a glorious battle before Boston!

GEN. WASH. — What! That handful of militia withstand the onslaught of veteran troops! This is indeed stirring news!

GREENE. — Ay, general, 2,000 of the best British troops were repeatedly repulsed by a smaller number of provincials, hungry and thirsty, armed with their rifles and fowling-pieces and clad in their homespun, country garbs; one half of the enemy were either killed or wounded!

GEN. WASH. — Splendid, splendid! General, you have lifted a fearful weight of doubt and solicitude from my heart. With a just cause and such men as these to defend it, the liberties of our country are safe! But let me hear the particulars, my dear general; where was the battle fought?

GREENE. — Before brave old Boston! On the night of the l6th our troops had taken possession of Bunker's Hill and thrown up a line of earth-works. At dawn the British discovered their position and made preparations for a general assault. The patriots were ordered to retain their fire until the red-coats were within thirty paces. Then, at the word "fire!" a tremendous volley burst forth and the assailants fell back in confusion. But they rallied and advanced within pistol shot, when another volley, more destructive than the first, threw them into confusion, and a retreat was ordered!

GEN. WASH. — Well, well, was that the end?

GREENE — Oh, no, general, they were rallied and a second time repulsed. Rifles, muskets and fowling-pieces were leveled against the royal troops, with deadly aim. The British commander, at one time, stood alone upon the field, all his officers being either killed or wounded. The carnage was terrible! The regulars fell back in dire disorder, some even rushing into their boats.

GEN. WASH —And then?

GREENE —And then, after a pause, the British again ascended the hill to storm the redoubt. Our men poured forth repeated volleys with the fatal aim of sharp-shooters. The British stood the first shock, but the second and third staggered them. In vain their officers threatened, implored, ay, even attempted to goad them on with their swords; the havoc was too deadly; whole ranks were mowed down they broke and fled!    GEN.    WASH. (*rising*). —Glory enough for a single day. And so, our men held the redoubt against them?

GREENE. —No, general, the enemy now perceived that we had exhausted our ammunition and orders were given to carry the earth-works at the point of the bayonet! Then ensued a desperate and deadly struggle, hand to hand, with bayonets, stones and the stores of muskets. Our soldiers retired slowly and in good order, disputing the ground inch by inch, undismayed, amid the thunder of artillery, the bursting of bomb-shells, the sharp discharges of musketry and the shouts and yells of the assailants.

GEN. WASH — Why, general, I shall have an army of veterans to take command of. But tell me, I beg of you, who were the brave officers that made our men do such brilliant service?

KNOX. —Ah! General, there was a host of them. The veteran Prescott and the dauntless Warren, brave old John Stark and glorious old Putnam, were there! Within ten minutes after the cry of blood rose from the field of Lexington, Stark was in his saddle, spurring towards Boston. And that grand old patriot Putnam hurried to Boston at the first news of British violence. The messenger found him in the field ploughing, assisted by his son. In an instant the team was unyoked, the plough left in the furrow, the lad sent home to give word of his father's departure, and the splendid old patriot, on horseback, in his working garb, urging with all speed to the camp at Bunker's Hill. He did glorious service. Riding about on that sultry day, with his sword buckled across his brawny shoulders, he was a leading spirit throughout the struggle. Calm amid the storm of battle, his voice cheered the men on like the sound of a trumpet. Sword in hand, he rode to the rear of our retreating troops, regardless of the balls whistling about him, and cried out to them: "Halt! Make a stand here. We can check them yet. In God's name, form and give them one shot more!"

GEN. WASH. — Brave old man! I heard of him years ago. He is a true patriot, honest and fearless, and if God spares his life will yet do glorious service for his country. I long to grasp the old farmer by the hand. We shall need such men for, believe me, there is no retreat for us now but that which leads to shame and dishonor. And think you our countrymen will ever tread that path?

GREENE and KNOX. — Never, general, never!

GEN. WASH. — I pray heaven they never may! But their souls will be sorely tried, for proud England is a stubborn foe, and will wring dear blood from dearest hearts ere the end shall come; and therefore, I am preparing to bid a long farewell to my beloved Mount Vernon. But, gentlemen, I crave your pardon. The glorious news you are bearers of made me quite forget that I am a farmer still and can give you a farmer's cheer (*rings*). I pray you go and refresh yourselves. I'll join you presently.

GREENE and KNOX. — Your servants, general.

GEN. WASH. — William, conduct the gentlemen to the dining-room. Let Christopher attend them, and you return to me.

## SCENE FIFTH.

GEN. WASH. (*solus*). — One thousand British soldiers killed and wounded! We are rebels now in earnest, and England's king will show us no mercy. Ay, and now the shades of our brothers fallen on the fields of Lexington and Concord cry unto us no more! We have given them sleep.

## SCENE SIXTH.

WM. (*re-entering*). The gemmen are at the table, gin'ral.

GEN. WASH —Ah, William, I forgot to tell you. I ride Valliant, you know; have you saddled him?

WM. —Yes, gin'ral.

GEN. WASH —Are his eyes bright —his hide sleek?

WM. —Ay, gin'ral, bright as buttons —slick as a ribbon. He has been callin' you fo' half an hour. I tole him all about leabin' ole Virginny fo' de norf he werry proud to dink dat you chewsed him out ob all de odders dey werry jealous, I tell you, gin'ral.

GEN. WASH. — Look well to the girths, William. And William—

WM. —Yes, gin'ral?

GEN. WASH —Don't let Valliant be alone; he might chafe himself against the tying-post.

WM. —No danger, gin'ral dat horse nebber cuts up no shines no how. I dink dat horse been to school somewhar, fo' shuah. Bress my soul, ef he only knewed his letters how he would speak right out and say: "Look out dar, William; don't rub me too hard wid dat curry comb."

GEN. WASH. — Oh, William!

WM —Yes, gin'ral.

GEN. WASH. — Is my mother in her apartments?

WM. — Yes, gin'ral; I dink she are, fo' shuah.

GEN. WASH — Say to her that I ask permission to pay my respects that I leave for the North at once —no, don't say that, William the first will do.

WM. —Yes, gin'ral [*going.*]

GEN. WASH —Poor lady! her heart is brave and strong, and yet 'tis hard to rob it of its peace and comfort.

WM. (re-*entering*). — Too late, gin'ral, too late —here comes Missus Washington now. (*Enter* MARY WASHINGTON.)

## SCENE SEVENTH.

GEN. WASH —Why, mother, how is this? 'Tis wrong in you. The stairway wearies you so much. I had this moment sent to say that I would wait upon you.

MARY. — Has not Mary Washington the right to wait upon her country's chief -the general of its armies?

GEN. WASH Were I ten times general, I am still your son!

MARY. Ay, more. Dear George, you never were a child. Man, from the first, you've been my trusted counsellor and staunch support.

GEN. WASH. —What I have been to you, Mother, I still shall be. Each week will bring you tidings from the North.

MARY. — Ah, George, your voice, your smile, your presence; these are light and warmth to my aged heart. I am too old to live on hope my son, my son! I ne'er may look upon your face again!

GEN. WASH. — Oh say not so, Mother! Think of the past and its adieux, and how I came each time, from ocean, camp and wilderness, in safety back to home again.

MARY. —The dangers, then, were few, and in those days, I wore a stouter heart within my breast! But now, now — oh, George, my son. Will heaven ever let me clasp your hand again? [*Leads her to a seat.*]

GEN. WASH —Ay, mother, have no fear; there's that within my heart tells me I'll come again. I do not seek to know what time alone can solve but from my boyhood, when in camp or forest, peril seemed most imminent and life locked arms with death and wrested for the mastery, the warm blood never left my cheek. I know not why, nor do I make my boast thereof, but when returning from Venango, thro' the wilderness, my guide, with sudden treachery, turned around and fired his rifle at my breast, I never quailed, but stood so firm and motionless that my companion thought me dead and when, upon the next ensuing day, embarked upon the Alleghany's flood, the ice fell fierce against our raft and hurled me headlong in the angry stream, no fear seized on my heart! The torrent, roaring in my ears, seemed like an old friend's voice, and stirred my blood until each sinew grew as strong as iron, and I was saved! And lastly, mother, when upon ill-fated Braddock's field, amid the shower of iron and leaden hail, the piteous cries of wounded men, and savage war-whoop loud above the din and roar, I calmly rode about and cheered our panic-stricken troops, with vain endeavor sought to stem the rout and hold the savage enemy in check, I never thought of fear the bullets pierced my clothes and killed two horses under me And when I saw our men turn from their guns and seek the woods for safety, I sprang from my horse, and wheeling round a field-piece toward the Indians, scattered death among their ranks! And still I stood unharmed upon that field of blood, so that the superstitious chiefs cried to their warriors: "Turn your rifles away, for the Great Spirit is protecting him!"

MARY. — Ah, George, my son, but now the times are changed. Then you were shielded by proud England's might. Now you've unsheathed your sword against your king.

GEN. WASH. —Nay, madam, nay! My king no more! The slight allegiance that I owed this monarch once his tyranny absolves me from forever.

MARY. — Oh, these are woeful, woeful days for wives and mothers' hearts! My boy, my boy, you know the strength of England's troops you know the power of England's gold, and what have we to lean upon except our honor and our God?

GEN. WASH. —Mother, we have the glorious consciousness that we are right, and if that cannot steel our hearts against all fear of England's gold and England's soldiery, then, truly, are we only fit to be King George's slaves.

MARY. — God send us help! And yet, my noble son, on your dear head will fall the royal wrath should England drive the patriot army from the field. You are the rebel chief! You are the leader of the patriots who have dared resent the measures of the English crown and fire upon the royal troops. Altho' there be forgiveness for the rest, there'll be for pardon for my son.

GEN. WASH — (*sitting down and taking her hand.*) Let no such thought give trouble to your heart. Mother, I know my countrymen if I am beaten in the north, it will avail them naught! The mountains of the west shall be my refuge then I know each path and road, each stream and valley. There the patriot chiefs will gather round me! Putnam, Knox and Greene, with Schuyler, Stark and Wayne, and there we'll make a desperate stand for freedom. Driven out from there, we'll cross the Alleghany ridge! The forest and the flood, the mountains and the wilderness shall be our allies. There we'll keep the fire of freedom burning on the mountain tops, and now and then rush down on our oppressors like an avalanche 'till England's mercenary hordes shall dread our very names!

MARY. — Amen! Amen!

GEN. WASH. — And now, my mother, fare you well! Oh, be assured I'll ever wear your image in my heart. Can I forget how much I owe your love? If I have aught in me that fits me for command, and gives me power o'er men, I learned it here! Your eyes, your voice, your manner taught it me! Ay here it was, here at your knees that I first learned to love the sacred cause for which I now unsheath my sword; and if I serve my native land with honor, lead my countrymen to victory or fall in glorious conflict for our rights, to you, Mother, be all the praise, to you be all the honor due.

MARY. — George, my son, my boy, a mother's blessing and a mother's prayer be ever with you till the end! Be firm, be good, be true!

GEN. WASH. — I will, I will! (*A trumpet sounds.*) Hark, there, Mother, my escort has arrived come, you shall waive your son a last adieu!

MARY. — Stay, George! Here are some faithful souls, who wait to speak their hearts' farewell, and cry, "Godspeed!" Come in, come, one and all. Here, faithful creatures, is the man whom you all love so well!

[*The slaves rush in and group about WASHINGTON, some kneel, some clasp his hands.*]

ALL. — Farewell, Massa Washington! Good bye! God bless you! Farewell, dear Massa! Good bye!

GEN. WASH. —Farewell! Farewell!

GREENE *and* KNOX *appear with their aids; also,* WILLIAM, *with W's hat and cloak.*

MARY. (*advancing and handing* WASHINGTON *his sword.*) Remember me!

GEN. WASH. —Mother!

*Curtain on Tableau.*

## END OF ACT THE FIRST.

*The scene may be drawn aside, disclosing Tableau of America's Guardian Angel descending and blessing* WASHINGTON.

## 1778.

## ACT SECOND.

# Valley Forge—Camp-scene in Winter—Daybreak—Sentinels posted in front—Snow Storm.

## SCENE FIRST.

SENT. (*sings*)

### I.

Tramping, tramping slowly to and fro,
Dreaming of the loved ones far away;
Watching, watching 'mid the falling snow,
Longing for the coming of the day.
[*Reveille sounds in distance.*]
(*Soldiers' Chorus within.*)
Don't ye hear the reveille?
Rouse ye, comrades everyone!
We shall march to victory,
With the noble Washington!

### II.

SENT. —

## SCENE SECOND.

*Enter* STEUBEN *at the head of an awkward squad.*
BARON. —Vun doo, vun doo! Halt! Himmelsacrament, vat for you valk on your

## SCENE THIRD.

1ST SOL. — Ha, ha, ha! The old Baron has got thro' swearing for this morning!

2ND SOL. —Hark ye, comrade. I thought the General had forbidden the use of profane language in the army?

1ST SOL. — So, he has, when you swear in English, but the Baron swears in French and German, and so he doesn't disobey orders!

2ND SOL. —Ha, ha! He is a kind-hearted, generous old man, anyway, and the boys only laugh when he swears at them.

PABSON (*outside*). — Salutation and greeting!

1ˢᵀ SOL. —Ha, ha! Here comes the rousin' gospel preacher.

2ᴺᴰ SOL. —Here comes the fighting parson!

*Enter Parson, with huge sword, rifle and pistols.*

## SCENE FOURTH.

PARSON. — Salutation and greeting to the soldiers of Gideon's Band! Remember our bonds!

ALL. — Good morning, parson, good morning. Hurrah for the fighting parson —hurrah for the rousin' gospel preacher!

PARSON. — Yea, verily; even as Gideon slew the Medianites and as Samson smote the Philistines, hip and thigh, so shall we fall upon the enemies of our country! Remember our bonds!

1ˢᵗ SOL. — What's the news, parson? Tell us the news.

PARSON. — Yea, verily! Remember our bonds! The Philistines are encamped within the walls of our fair city of Philadelphia! And the leaders thereof are feasting therein and filling their stomachs with savory dishes and richly-flavored meats and viands, that are exceeding pleasant and wholesome to the palate, yea, verily! But, be not cast down, oh Gideon's Band, for when they have eaten and drunken and are full, then, verily, in that self-same hour, shall come forth a man's hand and write upon the plaster on the wall: "Mene, mene, tekel, upharsin!" And this is the interpretation of the thing: Mene, mene! Ye Philistines, verily ye have awakened the wrong customer! Tekel! Ye are too light a weight to cope with him! Upharsin! Verily he will inflict grievous injury upon thy frontispiece!

ALL. — Ha, ha, ha! Hurrah for the fightin' parson! That's the talk, Parson Caldwell!

PARSON. —Yea, verily —remember your bonds! For though you be grown as lean-fleshed as the seven lean kine of Egypt, and taste defeat as bitter as the waters of Marah, yet shall ye smite the Hessians, the Hanoverians and the Brunswickers, even as Joshua smote the Hittites, the Jebusites and the Perizzites, even as Samuel smote Agag and hewed him in pieces at Gilgal! even as Jael smote the nail into the head of Sisera, so shall we smite England's tyranny under the fifth rib, and it shall die. Yea, verily —remember your bonds

ALL —Three cheers for the rousin' gospel preacher! Hurrah for the fighting parson! That's the talk, Parson Caldwell!

PARSON. — Yea, verily, remember your bonds! for I say unto you, brothers, that the British king commanded us to make bricks, yet gave us no straw, and sent task-masters over unto us, saying: Go, get your straw where you can find it yet not aught of your work shall be diminished! Yea, verily, King George hath hardened his heart, and the great city of London has become like Nineveh of old, wherein were more than six score thousand persons that could not discern between their right hand and their left -hand! Yea verily, remember your bonds!

ALL. — Ha, ha, ha! Hurrah for the rousin' gospel preacher —good, good; that's the talk, parson —pitch into 'em, give it to 'em!

PARSON. —Yea, verily, remember your bonds for our enemies have hardened their hearts and will not listen unto the words of wisdom and reason, and therefore I say unto you, take pages from the proverbs of Solomon, and leaves from the pages of Dr. Watts, and use thereof for wad, that in the end we may shoot wisdom and good understanding into the hearts of our enemies! Yea, verily, brethren, remember your bonds.

ALL —Ha, ha, ha! good, good; that's the talk Parson Caldwell! Good for the fightin' parson we'll give 'em Dr. Watts we'll shoot the proverbs into 'em! Ha, ha, ha!

3$^{RD}$ SOL. — Ho, there comrades! Peace! Peace! The general is coming this way! Fall back! Fall back!

1$^{ST}$ SOL. —No, no, stand fast, comrades! The general loves his children, and likes to have them about him. Long live George Washington!

PARSON. — Yea, verily, remember your bonds! But be not cast down, and raise not up your voices in sore a bitter lamentation, for verily I say unto you, that even Joshua cried out in the sight of Israel: Sun, stand thou still upon Gibeon, and Moon stay thou in the valley of Aijalon, so even hath George Washington cried unto England's king: "King, thou shalt rule no more over us. Depart, thy tyranny is ended forever!"

ALL. — Hurrah! Hurrah! Hurrah! Good for the fightin' parson —good for the rousin' gospel preacher. Three cheers for Parson Caldwell. Ha, ha, ha!

1$^{ST}$ SOL. — See, comrades, the general's sweet wife is with him! God bless Martha Washington!

ALL. — So say we all!

PARSON. — Amen! So mote it be. Remember our bonds.

1ST SOL. — Fall back, comrades; fall back, I say. They'll pass this way. Fall back, there.

2ND SOL. — No, no; Martha Washington loves the soldiers, too.

3RD SOL. — Ay, ay she braves the hardships of Valley Forge to cheer us up. God bless her!

*Enter* WASHINGTON *with his wife and generals.*

## SCENE FIFTH.

ALL. — Hurrah! Hurrah! Hurrah          (*Music.*)

1ST SOL.— Long live General Washington!

2ND SOL. — Long live our brave commander! (*Cheers.*)

1ST SOL. (*to a country maiden*). —Fall back, there, woman! Where are ye goin'? Haven't ye any manners?

MAIDEN. (*to Mrs. W.*). — Please, gracious lady, deign to read this paper. Good lady, please help a poor girl.

MARTHA. — Don't kneel to me, good woman. What can I do for you?

MAIDEN. — Oh, I'm over head and ears in trouble, generous lady. This is my Ebenezer, and please, madam, the officer says he will not grant no leave of absence to no man, no how. (*Weeps.*)

[MARTHA *hands petition* to Gen. W.]

MARTHA. — Poor woman George, may not her prayer be granted?

GEN. WASH. —I hope it may, my gentle wife, since you have pitied her. Gentlemen, I need a trusty counsellor to stand impartial in this matter.

LA F. — Choose me, dear general. I'll be firm and just.

GEN. WASH. — No, no, marquis, you are too young. What answer could you make to all these tears? Come baron, your soldier's heart is well entrenched and strongly garrisoned. I refer the petition to you.

BARON (*advancing*). —Vell, yoman, vat you vant?

MAIDEN. — Please, sir, this is my Ebenezer?

BARON. — *Parbleu*, I have been got vell acquainted mit him, he tidn't knowed his right hand foot from his left. Vell, vat vill you make mit your Ebenezer?

MAIDEN. — Please, good sir, I want to take him home with me. We were going to be married three months ago, but Ebenezer, he got his dander up.

BARON. — Vat, vat —vat —vat vas dat peen, hey?

MAIDEN. — I mean, he got all fired mad at me 'cause I danced with Aminadab Crane at Mehitable Johnson's apple peelin', and so —and so —he went —he went —and 'listed as a soldier-boy —he did —to —to break my heart.

BARON. —Vell, if he make not loaf besser als he make de soldier, I advised you took de odder man.

MAIDEN. — Please, sir, marm said as how I was sure to bring him back with me, as how the cider was gettin' too hard to drink, and pop said as how Ebenezer might come back to his company after two, or three, or four or five months.

BARON. — Mein goodness gracious, woman, tidn't he have got a country to fight for, hey?

MAIDEN — Please, sir, I know my Ebenezer will fight better for his country when he has a wife to fight for, too.

BARON — Oh, took him along. I cannot talk mit a voman!

SOLDs. — Ha, ha, ha, ha!

MAIDEN — God bless you, sir. God bless you. You shall have a piece of the wedding cake, sir. Come, Ebenezer.

EBEN —Long life to you, sir!

SOLDS. —Long live Baron Steuben! Ha, ha, ha!

*Enter* HAMILTON.

## SCENE SIXTH.

HAM. — General, our scouts bring us important news.

GEN. WASH. — From Philadelphia?

HAM. — Yes, general, the enemy are preparing to evacuate the city!

GEN. WASH. — Thank Heaven for this bloodless victory! Now, gentlemen, we've work upon our hands! The winter's over, the hills will soon be green again, the highways flee from ice and snow. Nature no longer wars upon us! Come, let's pledge anew our lives, our fortunes and our sacred word, that England ne'er shall rule this land again and let our war-cry be: "Our country must and shall be free!" And if the British dare re-cross the Jersey plains embarrassed with their cumbrous baggage trains, we'll fall upon their flank and strike them such a grievous blow that all the sorrows of this dreary camp shall be that day forgot. Meanwhile, dear marquis, with two thousand of our chosen men, approach the city, rout their plundering bands, and when their army moves, press hard upon their rear! Be cautious, be alert, and keep me well-advised of all! Remember, La Fayette, my friend, two worlds are watching you!

LA F. — My dear commander, be assured I shall do my duty like a soldier, and if need be, die like one! Farewell!

GEO. WASH. —Farewell, and God be with you!

VOICES (*outside*). — Hurrah! Hurrah! Long live General Arnold! Long live the gallant leader!

GEO. WASH. — What? Arnold? Do they not cry! Long live Arnold? Surely the wounded soldier does not come to share with us the miseries of Valley Forge?

GREENE. —Ay, general, here he comes, dragging his wounded limbs along!

Enters ARNOLD *on crutches, pale and haggard.*

## SCENE SEVENTH.

GEO. WASH. (*advancing*). — Arnold I'm joyed to see you on your feet again, but fear you've ventured forth too soon! Your sword has carved a glorious record, you must live to keep it ever bright and pure!

ARNOLD. — My dear commander, need I tell you how a soldier's spirit chafes and galls beneath enforced response? But when thereto you add neglect, you give the nettle double sting!

GEN. WASH. — Ah, friend! Is that wound open yet? I swear to you, you have no cause to murmur thus. Your wrongs are all imaginary; think no more of them. Does not your country love and honor you. Ay, name you among her sons best loved? Be generous as you are brave; for by high heaven, Arnold, I'm your friend. And he my enemy who dares to say there lives a braver, truer man than you!

ARNOLD. — Dear general, were wrongs piled triple-deep upon my heart, your words would sweeten all the gall they could press out! You know I love my country well, and tho' my countrymen scoff at my services and say my wounds were got by chance, I swear they shall not sour me into discontent! I say I love my country, and with her I rise or fall!

GEN. WASH. — Arnold, I never doubted you, but still, lest evil tongues say that mine actions war upon my words, I have determined thus! The royal troops —so do our scouts report — have roused themselves at last and shaken off the stupor of their winter's rest. This means retreat without a shot against our works. But they shall not escape me thus! I'll strike them ere they reach New York. You shall command the left wing of my army, battle by my side and share the glory of the day.

ARNOLD — Ah, General my noble, generous friend, I love my country, but look on me now and say, when I shall mount my horse again.

GEO. WASH. —Arnold, I know your heart as well as tho' I wore it in my breast! I see, my friend, what British lead, and all the hardships that attend on war, have wrought upon your frame! But I can stir the old fires till thy blaze again! For I can cry: "See, Arnold, see, the British drive our men before them? Throw yourself upon their flank, roll up their line and save the day!" Come life, come death, you'd cast your crutches 'way, forget your wounds and leap upon your horse in answer to my call.

ARNOLD — Ah! Dear commander, yes; you're right, I say. I love my country, but my fighting days are past —perhaps forever past —for blood is blood! I've emptied all my vigor out! I was, perhaps, a little reckless, too; for scores of times, so has my spirit boiled and raged to see those hirelings shooting down my men, that with a blood-hound's fury I have rushed upon their ranks, and felt myself more like a beast than man, so did I thirst for blood! But then I loved my country, and I knew that I must rise or fall with her. Discretion flew to all the winds! But now, my dear commander, look upon my face; I am not what I was. I'm broken, am I not, from too much use? But still I say I love my country, and with her I rise or fall! But now, I must have rest — rest — rest!

GEN. WASH. — Rest, Arnold, rest? There will be rest for none until our work is done and England's king says we are free! Rest, Arnold, rest was that your word? By Heaven, sir, had other lips said, "Arnold asks for rest," I would have thought they lied!

ARNOLD. — And yet I love my country, dear commander. You know that; but blood is blood! No doubt I've been a little reckless now and then. It was no fault of mine but of the cause I love to serve —the glorious cause of liberty! And now I ask for rest Until my vigor comes again, and I can cast aside these helps and be myself once more.

GEN. WASH — It is accorded, sir. You have the right to ask for rest. I will be just You are entitled to it; go, my friend, regain your health and strength. Then bring your sword to me, and I will give you work, Arnold.

ARNOLD. —Why, general —sir, you wrong me. I do not desire such rest as that. You wrong me, sir. Inglorious indolence! I'd rather die than rest like that! Give me some post to guard, a garrison command somewhere, that calls for sleepless watchfulness! You know, my dear commander, no one loves his country more than I; and this my country hath of late Herself confessed. Is not my horse the gift of Congress? Ay, and these the epaulets your hand bestowed on me? They are the badge of your regard and confidence. I feel my heart beat lighter while I have them on. I therefore ask, if you do still confide in me, some quiet post of — say, West Point. The mountain air will soon restore my health. In truth, that mountain fastness is a post of honor. 'Tis our Gibraltar rock. To Freedom's column, Nature's pediment! To lose it would imperil —I almost had said —bring death to Freedom's holy cause.

GEN. WASH. — Ay, Arnold, that is true! that's very true!

ARNOLD. — But, dear commander, why, if you would have me nearer you, why, then some other post—

GEN. WASH. —No, no, no, Arnold; no! Of late my thoughts have clung with a strange persistency to this important post of ours. Our scouts report of late large reinforcements to the British troops within New York. They'd strike a desperate blow to gain West Point, if but success with faintest glimmer beckoned on. I cannot sleep so do these thoughts oppress my mind. My friend, I'm glad you've asked me for't I'm very glad. 'Twill give me peace of mind to know that you command this post of ours. So, then, dear Arnold, rest your wounded limbs and be content. West Point is yours!

ARNOLD (*aside*). —At last!

*Noise and confusion outside.*        *Enter* OFFICER.

## SCENE EIGHTH.

OFF. — A dangerous mutiny has broken out among the troops. They've seized their arms, and demand an audience with the Commander-in-Chief!

GREENE. — Insolence! Are my Rhode Island troops among the mutineers?

OFF. — No, sir; not a man.

GREENE. — Then all is well! General, give me leave, and I will quell this mutiny with an iron hand.

GEN. WASH. — Sir, what is the cause of this outbreak?

OFF. — The old one, general, hunger! Our supplies failed yesterday. Our men are crazed from cold and destitution. 2,000 out of 11,000 are sick or helpless from frozen hands or limbs. They incite the rest to acts of desperation. Yet the mutineers have not harmed their officers; but no one can tell how long their forbearance may endure.

2ND OFF. (*entering*). The revolt is spreading; the Eastern troops threaten to join the mutineers; our camp is in disorder and confusion; they warn their officers not to interfere! Their cry is! "Let us march to the general's headquarters!"

GREENE. — This is infamous, general.

GEN. WASH. — I'll go and talk with them!

MARTHA. —Oh George, I implore you, do not risk your life. The troops are maddened to despair —they might forget themselves!

GREENE. —At least, dear general, go armed (*offers his pistols*).

GEN. WASH. —Not even with this! (*hands his sword to an aid*). I'll fight them with the love they bear me!

1ST OFF. — Here they come! Here they come!

2ND OFF. —Be careful, general let me call your guards!

[*The soldiers rush in.*]

## SCENE NINTH.

SOLDIERS —Bread! Bread! Justice! Justice!

(ARNOLD *seizes his crutches in one hand and rushes forward.*)

GEO. WASH. —Halt!

1ST SOL. —General, we come for bread!

2ND SOL. —We'll fight, but we will not starve.

3RD SOL. —Give us our rights we demand them!

GEN. WASH. —Silence! Throw down your arms, or I will not hear you speak (*They obey.*)

OLD SOLD. (*advancing*). — You see, general, we stand with our hearts, and not our weapons in our hands! Look upon me! I am an old man, whose breast and limbs are scarred from forty years' hard service against the French and Indians. I stood beside you on Braddock's bloody field, and saw you ride unharmed amid that storm of leaden hail —and I loved you. Do we not all love you? These are my poor comrades my children, as I call them. But must we starve, freeze, die from want and exposure I am a poor old man. I left a son at Bunker's Hill, another on Saratoga's field, and here (*pointing to a bier which they advance*) lies my third boy, whom I dragged from his mother's arms four years ago.

[G. W. *covers him with his cloak.*]

OLD SOL. —Ah dear commander, that cloak of all others in this world would warm my boy's heart, but now it is too late, for he is dead!

GEN. WASH. —Dead!

OLD SOL. Ay, dead, from cold and hunger!

GEN. WASH. (*uncovering —all do likewise. The parson kneels*): Oh Father, hear, we call upon Thy name. For these are heavier blows than England strikes. Let not despair brood o'er this wintry camp. And shut the cheerful light of Heaven out. Oh, give us hearts to hear these things, and make us worth of the sacred cause we serve.

PARSON. — Amen! So, mote it be! Yea, verily! Remember your bonds, oh soldiers of Gideon's band! (*A pause.*)

## SCENE TEN.

*Enter Messenger.*

MESS. —Important dispatches for the commander-in-chief.

GEN. WASH. — Read, Hamilton.

HAM. — Here's glorious news, general! The king of France has sent a fleet and men to our assistance!

[*The soldiers cheer and toss their hats.*]

PARSON (*very loud*). — Halleluiah! Halleluiah! Remember your bonds!

GEN. WASH — Heaven be praised and La Fayette be thanked for this.

ARNOLD (*aside.*) — A despot for an ally! And yet they call this a contest for freedom!

GEN. WASH. —Return to your quarters, men. Your wants shall be relieved at once. Be patient and all will yet go well.

[*They cheer.*]

(*To his officers.*) To horse, gentlemen!

[*He passes out leading his wife by the hand his generals follow.*]

SOLDS. — Long live George Washington! long live the king of France hurrah, &c.

[Cannon, music, cheering.]

ARNOLD (*aside*). — And so, the sacred cause of freedom will be polluted by a tyrant's sword!

PARSON. (*singing and dancing*). —Yea, verily, brothers, sound the sackbut, psaltery and dulcimer! Strike the cymbals and blow the trumpets; lift your voices and be exceeding glad, for verily, verily the tidings from be yond the seas are full of joy and gladness! Remember your bonds!

SOLDS. — Hurrah, hurrah for the rousing gospel preacher, hurrah for the fighting parson! Ha! ha! ha!

PARSON —Yea, verily, brothers! now we'll make it hotter for the English king than Nebuchadnezzer did for Shadrach, Meshach and Abednego! Yea, verily!

SOLDS. — Ha! Ha! Ha! Good, good, that is the talk, parson. Ha! Ha! Ha!

*Re-enter WASHINGTON on horse followed by his generals and body-guard.*

## SCENE ELEVENTH.

SOLDs. — Long live George Washington! Long live our dear commander! Hurrah! Hurrah! Hurrah!

[*Cannon and music.*]

GEN. WASH. (*to Arnold*). —Arnold, I'll send you more men! Farewell! Heaven protect you and West Point.

PARSON. —Amen! so mote it be! yea, verily, remember your bonds!

[*Washington and his generals ride out amid the cheers of his men, the firing of cannon and waving of hats.*]

End of act the 2nd, or scene may be withdrawn and tableau of "*Washington crossing the Delaware,*" disclosed.

# 1780.

## ACT THREE.

### BEVERLY MANOR HOUSE, WEST POINT.

#### SCENE FIRST.

*A breakfast-room looking out upon the river. Mrs. Arnold arranging flowers.*

MRS. A. —Janet, I must have a French flag to place by the side of ours in this vase.

JANET. —I saw one lying on the mantel; yes, here it is, madam.

MRS. A. —Thank you, good Janet —there the lilies of France and the patriot colors are side by side. The gallant Marquis de La Fayette shall see that we thought of him.

JANET. — Dear madam, how your hand trembles!

MRS. A. — Good Janet, I'm weary before the day is begun.

JANET. — Twice last night, madam, you started up in your sleep clasped me around the neck and cried, "my child! my child!"

MRS A. — Ah yes, faithful Janet, it was a weary night for me. I dreamt someone had stolen my babe from me.

JANET. — How strange! But come, let me order up breakfast; you must eat something, dear mistress; it must be an hour before General Washington arrives.

MRS. A. — No, no; I'll wait for my husband, at least, why, 'tis past his hour now. Hark Janet, I hear footsteps. I know them, too; they are his. (*Springing joyously forward.*) Benedict!

#### SCENE SECOND.

*Enter* ARNOLD.

ARNOLD — Why, Madge, what's the matter?

MRS. A. — Oh, nothing, only I'm so glad you've come, that's all. Why don't you kiss me? This is the first time you've seen me this morning, Benedict.

ARNOLD (*kissing her*). — There, there, there, you're a good child; go.

MRS. A. — Shall we wait breakfast any longer, Benedict?

ARNOLD —Yes, wait.

MRS. A. — 'Tis past the hour General Washington named in his message to us. Have you been over the fortress this morning, Benedict? You look so tired. Let me order a cup of coffee for you.

ARNOLD — No, I want nothing. Janet?

JANET. — General.

ARNOLD — Remove those flowers.

MRS. A. — Benedict.

JANET — Why, general, our lady arranged them with the greatest care.

ARNOLD — Take them away, their odor oppresses me.

(*She leaves the flags.*) No, no, them too. You may go.

MRS. A. —Benedict, are you not feeling well? Has anything gone wrong?

ARNOLD —Why, Madge! Ha! Ha! Ha! What an idea. I'm well enough, come now, don't look so earnest, sweet Madge. Janet provoked me with her flowers and flags.

MRS. A. — Why, Benedict, I —

ARNOLD — There, there, Madge, never mind the flowers. Come, don't look so serious; I have not heard you laugh, I have not seen you smile, this morning. There, there, you are chiding me with your eyes again. Now, that's better; that's more like my gentle Madge.

MRS. A. — Dear husband, please God that I should never grieve you. Come, let me lay your hat and gloves aside. (*Arnold starts upon seeing that he has forgotten to remove them.*) You will surely not cross to the Point until after breakfast. Benedict! Husband! (*Arnold stands plunged in thought.*) (*Aside.*) Merciful Heaven! what has happened to him? He did not hear me speak. (*Loud.*) Benedict!

ARNOLD (*startled*). — Well, well, well, Madge I'm here. I'm here, my darling; all will yet go well.

MRS. A. — All, Benedict? Why? What?

ARNOLD — Nothing, nothing, my child, my darling Madge, my sweet wife. Nothing at all, nothing at all. Ha! Ha! Ha! By the way, sweetheart, I have — I have news for you. There, there, now don't look at me as if — as if I had been — doing wrong! Madge, my darling, your friend Major John —Andre—

MRS. A. —What of him, Benedict?

ARNOLD — Oh, nothing —ha! —nothing at all — simply this! You admired him, and —and —I'm told his society is very attractive; that he is an accomplished gentle man —that he is a sincere friend of yours.

MRS. A. — Well?

ARNOLD — Oh, nothing, Madge, nothing, only — that we may see him before long.

MRS. A. — See him, Benedict? Why, where?

ARNOLD — Where, Madge, where? Why at New York, of course.

MRS. A. — At New York, Benedict? What do you mean? Has the government received news from England? Are we to have peace?

ARNOLD. — Peace, Margaret! Who speaks of peace?

MRS. A. — Why, husband, how else shall we see Major Andre at New York?  ARNOLD. — How else, how else, Margaret? (*Sinking up on a chair.*) (*Aside.*) Oh, God! I cannot tell her. (*To his wife.*) Come, come, be frank, my darling Madge; your friendship for Major Andre — that is — confess that you would be delighted.

MRS. A. — Benedict, what is this mystery? I implore you.

ARNOLD — Margaret, I am your husband. Come, come, true love casteth out all fear. If you love me, let your answer spring from your heart, not from your lips. There, there, darling Madge, there is no harm done. I know of your love for Major Andre.

MRS. A. — Benedict!

ARNOLD. — I love him myself —that is, from what I have heard of him. I don't chide you for it. I learned it from a hundred mouths in Philadelphia. You were young and beautiful, he the favorite of his general courted, petted, admired for his talents and bravery. It was very natural —ha! ha! ha! Madge, it was very natural that you should have captivated each other. I don't chide you for it. Madge, Madge, my sweet pet, you shall see your friend again soon, soon, ay, very soon.

MRS. A. — Benedict, Benedict, in Heaven's name, what do you mean? You are so changed —your voice, your manner. Look in my face, speak to me, tell me what you mean? Why do you talk to me of Major Andre?

ARNOLD — Hark you, Margaret, you cannot deceive me. I know of your love for John Andre; I have it from a hundred mouths, ay, from your own lips.

MRS. A. — Benedict, Benedict, I conjure you, as you are my husband, as you are the father of my child, have done with this cruel taunting.

ARNOLD — Take care. Margaret; don't anger me. Do you deny that you ever loved John Andre?

MRS. A. — Why should I deny what I freely confessed to you when you asked me to become your wife? You know the story of that love, Benedict — its joy and its despair, how I refused to follow Andre to New York. I showed you my heart; I let you gaze upon its wound, that you might judge whether I was worthy to be your wife. And oh, my brave, my generous husband, you trusted me, and only clasped me tighter to your breast. Then why do you call up these shadowy forms to haunt our peaceful home?

ARNOLD. — Why, why, why, Madge, why? (*Aside.*) Because I am a fiend.

MRS. A. — Calm yourself, Benedict I will not chide you. I will not reprove you; let us think of other things. Come, dear husband, I'll laugh and smile you shall have no more cause to say that I am sad and thoughtful; the name of John Andre.

ARNOLD. — (*clutching her by the arm*). — S-h— Margaret, are you mad? There is someone coming; that name might be overheard.

[*Goes towards door.*]

MRS. A. — Benedict, tell me, I beseech you, what has happened? What is the matter with you? Husband, speak to me—

ARNOLD. —S-h—.

## SCENE THIRD.

*Enter servant.*

SERVANT. —The Marquis de Lafayette!

ARNOLD —Ah, marquis, you have come at last!

LA F. —Good morning, general! Your servant, madam.

ARNOLD — Let breakfast be served at once!

MRS. A. (*advancing*). — Marquis, you are welcome to Beverley Manor.

LA F. — For which I thank you, Madame, altho' I'm bearer of regrets from General Washington.

ARNOLD (eagerly). —The general, marquis, has aught happened?

LA F. —Oh nothing, dear general, you know our commander's zeal. He made a halt a few miles below here to examine some redoubts. General Knox and Colonel Hamilton are with him; they request your good lady not to wait breakfast for them.

MRS. A. — Oh, this is most unkind I'll soundly reprimand the general for this. Pray be seated marquis, I hope your morning ride has given you a good appetite, for you see we have nothing but soldiers' fare to offer you.

LA F. — If this be soldiers' fare, I like the service better than ever.

MRS. A. — My dear marquis, if you wage war as gracefully as you pay a compliment, I'd like to fight against you myself.

LA F. — I'd surrender at discretion, dear lady, in order to be nearer the enemy!

MRS. A. — Take care, my gallant marquis, that would be desertion; and if you were ever recaptured, would be punished with death!

LA F. — Provided you did not execute me as a spy! Ha, ha, ha! But seriously, my dear friends, I have news for you. I have just returned from Hartford, where our beloved commander had an interview with the French officers. He made an easy capture of their hearts, as I had anticipated. In truth, be is the realization of a young soldier's dream —hero and patriot, brave and incorruptible. Oh, I shall never forget that scene at Hartford! I wish, my dear Arnold, you could have witnessed it. How those countrymen of mine, as if with one impulse, refused to make use of a soldier's salutation, but bared their heads when George Washington stood before them! They felt within their hearts that they were in the presence of one of heaven's warrior-prophets sent to warn the kings of earth, and smite them if they disobey.

MRS. A. —My dear marquis, I don't wonder at your enthusiasm, for when I witness the love and devotion with which our men and officers cling to their commander, I almost wish I had been born a man, that I might have served him, and shared their joy! For be assured, my dear marquis, I count myself in nothing happier than in the love he bears my husband!

ARNOLD (*aside*). — Oh, God!

LA F. — Ay, dear lady of his deep and earnest affection for your husband, none knows better than I! Nay, nay, Arnold, don't turn your face away; be proud of it. At times when he praises you, I feel the warm blood rush to my face; for we are jealous of each other, dear madam. But, my friends, what stirs my heart most, is the rapturous delight with which the people receive the general when he enters their towns and villages. Our return from Hartford, two days ago, as we entered the suburbs of a town at nightfall, the whole population sallied forth to meet us. Men and women waved their handkerchiefs, and showered their blessings on our dear commander, while crowds of children carrying torches, pressed around us! There was no driving the little patriots away, until they had touched the hand of their father, as they called him. I was riding beside the general, and saw the tears, gather in his eyes. Suddenly he turned to me, and with that warm grasp of the hand he knows so well how to give, exclaimed! La Fayette, we may be beaten by the English, it is the chance of war, but there is the army they will never conquer!

ARNOLD (*clutching at his throat*). —Madge! Madge! Water, water!

MRS. A. — Merciful heaven, Benedict, what's the matter!

ARNOLD. —Oh, nothing, nothing; only a little vertigo. There, there, I'm better now. Be seated, my dear marquis, be seated I crave forgiveness for alarming you.

(*Enter servant.*)

SERVANT. — General, there's a messenger below with a letter, which he has orders to deliver into your hands; shall I admit him?

ARNOLD — No, no; I'll go to him, I'll go to him.

LA F. —Stay, Arnold, stay; receive your messenger here; meanwhile, with madam's permission, I'll ride down to the redout below, and learn the cause of the general's delay, for I see your good lady is determined to eat nothing until he arrives!

MRS. A. — You have my leave marquis, for I perceive that you are too good a soldier to even exercise your appetite without command.

LA F. —A soldier cannot be too cautious in the presence of the enemy! Au revoir! [*Goes.*]

## SCENE FOURTH.

MESS. (ARNOLD — *at the door*). — Let me pass, I say! Where's General Arnold? Ah, general, pardon me, but my orders were to deliver this letter into no one's hands but yours.

ARNOLD. —Yes, yes, yes; go, go, go! You see I have it —I have it!

*[Servant goes.] (Tears the letter open, and staggers backward to a chair.)*

My God! I'm ruined! I'm ruined!

MRS. A. — Benedict, Benedict; in heaven's name what has happened? Speak to me, speak to me! Oh, my husband! On my knees, I implore you!

ARNOLD. — Madge, Madge! Don't touch me; don't come near me. You are an angel and I am a fiend! I have dishonored you. I have set the mark of shame and infamy on you and our child. You'll call down the curse of heaven on me when I tell you what I have done

MRS. A. — Benedict, my husband, have mercy on me, have mercy on me!

ARNOLD. — Oh, God, have mercy on me, Margaret, for you will have none when I tell you all I have betrayed my country and must fly for my life! Margaret, Margaret, your husband is a traitor, and if captured will perish on the gallows.

MRS. A. — Benedict Arnold a traitor? It is false; it cannot be! You are delirious; you know not what you say. Your reason has fled! There is no love, no thought, no soul in your eyes. Merciful heaven, he is mad!

ARNOLD. — Would to God it was true. But no, Margaret; I'm a traitor, and the friends that worked my ruin have abandoned me. My messenger has been captured, and even this moment Washington may know of my plan to surrender West Point to the royal troops!

MRS. A. — Oh, Father in Heaven, I call upon Thee, for this is more than I can bear!

*[Reels, and is about to fall.]*

ARNOLD (*clasping her in his arms*). — Come, Margaret, nerve yourself. There is no time to be lost. A British sloop of war is at Verplanks. Let us take our child and seek safety beneath the English flag.

MRS. A. — Never!

ARNOLD. — Have a care, Margaret you are my wife and owe me obedience! You shall follow me to the English lines!

MRS. A. — Never.

ARNOLD. — You are right, Margaret. You love the country I have betrayed! I will not drag you down with my infamy, Margaret. I release you from your plighted word. You are my wife no more!

MRS. A. — Benedict!

ARNOLD — Farewell, Margaret, farewell forever!

*[Rushes wildly out.]*

MRS. A. — Benedict, Benedict! Husband, husband! (*She strives to follow him, but falls fainting to the floor, then rises bewildered.*) Where am I? What has happened? Benedict, are you there? Merciful heaven, he is gone! Benedict, Benedict! Husband, husband, come back! I'll forgive you, Benedict &c.

*[Staggers out of the room.]*

Enter WASHINGTON hurriedly, followed by LA FAYETTE, KNOX and HAMILTON.

## SCENE FIFTH.

GEN. WASH. — How is this, marquis? The house seems deserted. What has become of Arnold?

LA F. — I am at loss to explain his absence, general. I left him and his wife here but a few moments ago.

GEN. WASH. — Strange, very strange. Ring for a servant, Hamilton.

LA F. — Ah, now it occurs to me, general, that Arnold was complaining of a sudden illness when I left him.

GEN. WASH. — That may be the explanation, marquis. (*To the servant.*) Well, General Arnold, where is he?

SERV. — He left the house a few moments ago, sir, and rode towards the river. I think he has gone over to the fortress for inspection.

GEN. WASH. — Most likely. Inform his good lady of our arrival at once.

SERVANT. — She has withdrawn to her room, general, on account of illness, I think.

GEN. WASH. —Well, well, gentlemen, this is most unfortunate. Here we are without either host or hostess. But pray be seated, for tho' Arnold fights like a lion yet he lives like a lord. But see, our good friend La Fayette must have breakfasted on smiles and fine phrases. There stands his cup of coffee untasted. Ah, you young men are all in love with Mrs. Arnold.

LA F. — My dear general, do you not recollect a certain young Virginian colonel who once loitered in the path of duty; how a whole afternoon passed away like a dream; how the horses were countermanded, and he was not in the saddle until the next morning; how—

GEN. WASH. — My dear marquis, I surrender, I surrender. I didn't imagine you had such heavy artillery.

OTHERS. — Ha, ha, ha!

[*Enter messenger breathlessly.*]

## SCENE SIXTH.

MESS. — Ah, general, thank God I've found you at last! On my way to Hartford I learned that you had left that city and were returning to West Point. I turned bridle to overtake you, but your change of route misled me.

GEO. WASH. — Well, well?

MESS. — Here are letters and papers from Colonel Jameson.

[*Hamilton takes them.*]

GEN. WASH — Has an attack been made? Have we been overpowered at any point?

MESS. — All I know is, general, an important capture has been made.

[*Goes.*]

HAM — Gracious heaven! Arnold has turned traitor!

GEO. WASH. — 'Tis false I say! 'Tis false as hell! I'll not believe the idle tale! Here are the proofs, my dear commander. Look upon them this is Arnold's hand!

GEN. WASH. — Now, by high heaven, I swear! This is some foul conspiracy to ruin my friend. I will not look upon the thing. I pray you, gentlemen, resume your seats, come, come, our breakfast is untasted yet.

LA F. — Dear general, I do entreat you, give me leave to read: "Arnold's accomplice, John Andre, the adjutant-general of the British army, has been captured within our lines, with plans of our fortress at West Point, concealed upon his person.

GEN. WASH. — Show me, show me the proof of this! Oh, heaven! I cannot read the lines they crawl across the page like serpents. Tell me, La Fayette, my friend, is this thing true — is this all true?

LA F. — Ay general, perchance far more than what is written here. Benedict Arnold has betrayed his country and deserted to the enemy!

GEN. WASH. — What, marquis, say you so? Lion-hearted Arnold, glorious hero of a hundred battles, idol of his troops, the young Republic's favorite chief, who but two years ago, when wounded, crippled and repulsed before Quebec's strong walls, to all my dread forebodings gave reply: "I'm in the way of duty, and I know no fear!" Oh no, no, no, it cannot be. This is some deep-laid plot of envious men to stain brave Arnold's fame!

LA F. — Ah, dear commander, would to heaven it were so! But no, here are the damning proofs of this most infamous design; these letters writ in Arnold's hand, these plans of West Point found concealed within the boots of this young British officer. Oh, sir, 'tis infamous, but it is true!

GEN. WASH. — Oh gracious heaven, was it then for this I shielded him from envy's poisoned shaft? Was it for this I trusted, honored, loved this man? Oh, Arnold, Arnold, say, what fiend of hell was throne so high in power, that he could work the downfall of your soul!

[*Hides his face in his hands.*]

Kind friends, I crave forgiveness. I have said that which I should have left unsaid. Dear Hamilton, give me your hand, and give your pardon with it.

HAM. — My dear commander —

GEN. WASH. — Nay, my friend, 'tis past, 'tis past. I was most rudely shaken! I had built upon this man, and first it seemed that all was lost when this staunch prop was knocked away! How could I tell that love, which twined and blossomed so around my heart, would fret and poison thus? But now, now, now I know 't! General Knox, cross over to the post, assume command; by nightfall you shall have more troops; post double sentries; let your men sleep on their arms! And, general, put none except Americans on guard to-night!

[*Knox salutes and retires.*]

Quick, Hamilton, he'll try to pass Verplanks, by heaven, we must not let him do 't! My horse is at the door —ride him: spare neither whip nor spur! Away! And if the traitor's barge attempts to pass our batteries, sink it! Make Arnold prisoner, dead or alive!

[*Hamilton salutes and retires.*]

*Enter* Mrs. ARNOLD, *followed by* JANET.

## SCENE SEVENTH.

MRS. A. — Merciful father, what do I hear!

JANET. — Dear lady, come away, I beseech you!

MRS. A. — No, no, Janet, let me go. I will speak to him. Oh, sir; look upon me. I am his wife! If not for my sake, then for his child! Sir, sir, by the love you bear your mother, by the love you bear my husband, recall that command! Don't murder your friend!

GEN. WASH. — Ay, madam, as he was my friend, I'll spare him; but as he is a traitor —no, not if he were my father!

MRS. A. — Oh God, my poor husband!

GEN. WASH. — Come, marquis, we must look to our prisoner. British gold and stratagem will attempt his release

*[Going.]*

MRS. A. — Marquis General! Hear me, hear me!

GEN. WASH. — Come, I say, marquis! Arnold the traitor may escape us, but if his conscience be not dead, it will smite him when he hears that John Andre has met the doom of a spy!

MRS. A. — (*rushing wildly towards them.*) John Andre a prisoner! John Andre a spy! Father in heaven, the mystery is solved! Break, break, break wretched heart!

*[Falls lifeless to the floor.]*

### END OF ACT THE THIRD.

Or, scene may be withdrawn and the "Battle of Monmouth" disclosed.

# 1780.

## ACT FOURTH.

**WASHINGTON'S HEADQUARTERS AT TAPPAN-QUAINT OLD ROOM. SENTINEL VISIBLE THROUGH THE WINDOW— A STORM IN PROGRESS.**

### SCENE FIRST.

WILLIAM *asleep near the fireplace. Enter* MARTHA WASHINGTON *with a night-lamp.*

MARTHA. — I cannot sleep, my thoughts are with the doomed Andre. I hear his voice above the wail of the storm, pleading for mercy, mercy! Oh, these are woful, woful times! What a dreary night is this, and yet it is John Andre's last night on earth! (*A noise.*) Who's there!

WM. — Why dat's me, Missus Washington! I'se waitin' fo' de gin'ral. I dink I was done gone snoozin' fo' shuah. De gin'ral's berry late to-night! Golly molly! Jis heah dat wind whistle up dat chimbly! Dre'ful cold up heah among de Yankees. I wish I was back in ole Virginny, I do, Missus Washington; snug back in deah ole Mount Wernon. Dre'ful cold up heah! Oh, Missus Washington?

MARTHA — What is it, good William?

WM. — Jis afo' you comed in, while I was done gone snoozin', I —I dreamt about dat —dat Major Andrew.

MARTHA. — Poor Andre!

WM. — Missus, I fought I seed his face all white, jis like a piece of chalk, an' I fought I seed de big drops rollin' down, down dose white cheeks; and I fought I heard him say to his mudder! Don' ye cry, mudder it 'ill be all right up dar in the bressed happy land, whar dey don't hab no shootin', no killin', no nonsense ob no kind." (*A knock*.) Oh, golly, molly, what's dat?

MARTHA — Be quick, William it may be a messenger from the general.

MRS. A. (at the door.) — Let me pass.

WM. —Hol' on dar, woman, hol' on, I say go roun' to de odder do' do you heah me, woman?

MRS. A. — Oh, let me pass. Here, take this money.

WM. — Look a heah, woman, you can't come in dis do' no how.

MARTHA —In heaven's name, William, who is she? what does she want?

WM. —She's a werry s'picious pusson, Missus Washington. I dink I'll call de guard.

MARTHA — Stay, I forbid it. Let me speak with her.

WM. — Take car', Missus, she'll fool you: she may be a man; don' ye send ne away, please: I don't like de looks ob her, no how: she's berry s'picious pusson.

[MARGARET *motions* WILLIAM *away.*]

MAR. — Go, William.

WM. (going). — Take car', Missus dese wimmin fokes aint what dey always 'pear to be sometimes.

## SCENE SECOND.

MRS. A. (*throwing off her disguise*). — Martha Washington! Thank God I have found you at last!

MARTHA. — Woman, speak, who are you?

MRS. A. — Oh, lady, the name I bear is cursed; I dare not breathe it!

MARTHA. — Gracious heaven, you are—

MRS. A. — Margaret Arnold!

SENTINEL (*outside*). — All is well.

MARTHA. — Margaret Arnold, unfortunate woman, how did you gain admittance here — how did you pass the sentries?

MRS. A. — Oh, madam, if my sorrows have touched your heart don't ask me how I gained admission here; but tell me quickly, I implore you, do I come too late? have they—have they shot him?

MARTHA —Shot him? merciful Father! What do you mean? Can it be that Arnold has been captured?

MRS. A. — Arnold, madam, Benedict Arnold is dead.

MARTHA. — Dead.

MRS. A. — Ay, lady, and buried; he died of treason and is buried beneath his own infamy; but his victim John Andre, speak madam; he still lives; I do not come too late?

MARTHA. — Alas! The sentence of death but awaits my husband's approval.

MRS. A. — Father in heaven, save him! Save him! Oh, it cannot be! The great commander, the pure, the noble Washington will never suffer this innocent man to die, for I swear to you, lady, he is innocent. He is the victim of Arnold's infamous plot.

MARTHA. — S-h, madam, the walls have ears! I dare not talk with you upon this subject. You must leave this place at once! The general may return at any moment. He would not admit you to his presence. I am his wife; I must not listen to what I dare not repeat to him!

[*Goes toward bell.*]

MRS. A. — Stay, my dear lady, but one moment, I beseech you. Do not fear me! I swear to you before heaven my heart is as pure and free from the blight of Arnold's treason as your own. I am an American! Your husband is the leader of my country's armies; he will hear me; he will not repulse me; his heart is as tender as his life is noble and pure! Fear naught, dear lady, you may listen to me — you may, you may!

MARTHA — In Heaven's name, unfortunate woman, who am I, that you should pour your sorrows out to me? I am a helpless woman, like yourself. My pity and my tears are all that I can give you!

MRS. A. — Oh, lay them at your husband's feet, and I will ask no more! Honored lady, think not it was a blind decree when heaven willed that you should become George Washington's wife! God forbid! You have a holy mission here on earth, to sway your husband's will towards mercy's side, lest by one thoughtless act he dims the luster of his glorious name; for if an act be not entirely just, the little wrong that's in it will fester and corrupt the whole! If Andre, clad in patriot's garb, crept within our lines, and wore the livery of liberty to serve a tyrant in, then he should die! But no! Oh no, it was not thus! This widow's son, as gentle as he is brave and honorable, was dragged within our lines against his will. He would scorn to commit an act that merited dishonorable death! And now, and now, my country, shamed by Arnold's treason, and angered by his escape, turns upon his helpless victim! Oh, rash insensate judgment that thinks to kill a noble soul by mere ignoble death! Andre! Andre! the tears of coming ages will be yours, as mine are now!

[*She sinks upon her knees beside Martha Washington; a miniature falls upon the floor unseen by her. Martha Washington picks the miniature up.*]

MARTHA. — Gracious heaven, madam, speak! What is the meaning of this miniature? You turn pale; speak, can it be?

MRS. A. — Aye, lady, speak the word; fear nothing, it will not startle me! I do love this doomed man, and I am loved by him.

MARTHA. — Margaret Arnold! You, a wife, a mother, confess you love this British officer! God pity you, for now the world will never acquit you of your husband's crime! His infamy will cling to you! They'll say you were the go-between and lent your grace and beauty to ensnare this vain and giddy man for your husband's infamous uses! God pity you, I say, for the world will show you no mercy! Would I could recall the tears I've shed! Oh, leave me, leave me! I order it; for I despise you!

MRS. A. — Stay! Stay, madam; on my knees I entreat you, hear me.

MARTHA. — No, no! it must not be! I'll hear no more. Farewell, and God help you!

[*Going.*]

MRS. A. — (*drawing a dagger.*) Martha Washington, another step, and I'll kill myself at your feet!

MARTHA. — Forbear!

SENTRY (*outside*). — All is well!

MARTHA. — Rash, impetuous woman, what would you at my hands?

MRS. A. — Justice!

MARTHA. — Look to heaven for that!

MRS. A. — Aye, lady, in good time. But you condemn me ere you hear me speak.

MARTHA. — Bethink yourself, madam, where you are, and the hour it is. If you have aught to say, off, say it quickly, and be gone!

MRS. A. — God bless you, honored lady, for that permission! Oh, do not turn away! I do not fear your gaze. Look in my face while I speak, and then you will believe me! (*A pause.*) Three years ago, the British troops driving our army before them, took possession of Philadelphia and our poor soldiers, naked and hungry, withdrew to Valley Forge; that dreary camp, whose hardships you shared with your illustrious husband. I lived at my father's home he stood neutral, but I was heart and soul a patriot! The British soldiers were wont to rally and call me "Fair Rebel Madge," while I retorted with: "Sir Myrmidon," or "Gentle Hireling." Among them was John Andre. I liked him not at first. I deemed him a heartless trifler, who loved for pastime. But one day as I read to him of the sufferings at Valley Forge of our patriot soldiers, dragging their bleeding feet over the crusted snow, I saw the tears gather in his eyes, and then I loved him. But the end came soon. He asked me to become his wife, and follow the royal army to New York. I refused, and bade him wait till peace should come. He chided me harshly, and roiled my haughty spirit, so we parted. Since then I have not seen his face. And now the patriot army came, and with it Arnold! I long had wished to see this man, the lion-hearted, "the mad, brave Arnold," so they called him. His pale face and deep-set burning eyes made me tremble when he spoke my name. There was a strange, mysterious power about the man; voice, manner, gaze told of the whirlwind chained within. But I was faithful to myself, and let him know the secret of my heart. I confessed my love for Andre in true and earnest words. But Arnold laughed away my fears, called it "school girl's fancy," said "he'd trust my heart," and I loved him for trusting me. And so, we reach the bitter end. Husband, country, honor, all are lost! There's nothing left save infamy and shame.

MARTHA. (*holding out her arms*). — And my belief in your innocence!

MRS. A. — God bless Martha Washington. Then you do pity me, dear lady, and you will entreat your husband to be merciful and spare the life of this poor widow's son! I know you will. I see it in your eyes! You'll whisper mercy in his ear, so soft and sweet, he'll think some angel murmurs it. Oh, father, I thank thee! A flash of hope illumes my heart! Andre may yet be saved!

SENTRY (*outside*). — Turn out the guard.

MARTHA. — My husband! Quick, madam, follow me! If he learns of your presence here, all hope is dead! Keep up a stout heart, I'll come again

[*Conducts her to side room.*]

MRS. A. — Oh, Heaven, be merciful.

VOICE (*outside*). — Present arms!

Enter WASHINGTON.

## SCENE THIRD.

## SCENE FOURTH.

HAM. — I bring the report of the Board of Officers. Your instructions were to lay it before you the moment I received it.

GEN. WASH. — I thank you, Hamilton! What's their verdict?

HAM. (reading). — That Major John Andre, Adjutant General to the British army, ought to be considered as a spy from the enemy, and that agreeably to the law and usage of nations, it is their opinion he ought to suffer death.

SENTRY (outside). — All is well!

[*Martha sinks upon a chair, and hides her face in her hands.*]

HAM. — Will your excellency affix your approval to the report to-night?

GEN. WASH. — Leave it, Hamilton, and return to me at a later hour.

[Wash. sits; Martha at his feet. Hamilton salutes and retires.]

## SCENE FIFTH.

MARTHA. —Oh, George! George! Heaven be your guidance in this fearful hour! Be not precipitate. Remember who it was conceived this most unholy wrong —your trusted friend! But heaven hath snatched him from your wrath. He is beyond your reach, and not the death of twenty Andres can add a single torment to his soul! Beloved, I know the many virtues that do dwell within your noble heart! Oh, let it ne'er be said of you, that mercy, the divinest of them all, was lacking there!

GEN. WASH. — Ay, Martha, noble wife, 'tis godlike to forgive; but I have hearts of flesh and blood to battle with! Poor, weary human hearts that have within them garnered up such strong remembrance of the grievous tyranny of England's king —whose breast is flint, else we had softened it with prayers and tears —that if I talked to them of mercy now, I'd lose the flood-gates of the people's rage (and spite of all their love for me) be caught up in the torrent, and to my destruction hurled! Or else, they'd cry: "Remember Nathan Hale!" And who does not remember him, and how he met his death within the British lines. Refused religious comfort, and denied the use of bible; all his letters to his mother burned before his eyes, and yet he spoke no word, save to lament that he could die but once, for his dear native land!

MARTHA. — Brave heart! He faced an ignominious death to serve his country, and he fell! 'Twas hard, 'twas terrible, but it was just! In deep disguise he left New York, and passed within the British lines! He was a spy!

GEN. WASH. (*rising*). — In deep disguise, John Andre strove to pass without our lines! He was a spy!

MARTHA. — At very worst, a messenger, no more.

GEN. WASH. — At very best, a messenger of infamy! Dispatched with British gold, to buy what British steel could not effect.

MARTHA. — He is so young to die!

GEN. WASH. — He was far better dead, then live to deal with men who sell their native land!

MARTHA. — He is a widow's son!

GEN. WASH. — Thank God, there'll be but one gray head to bend in sorrow to the grave!

MARTHA. — Oh, hear me, noble husband, hear! You know the love I bear you! Hear me heed my words. This death will stain the spotless record of your life. Reflect, beloved! At least, speak to your countrymen! Cry "Mercy" unto them, and with a gesture of command, awe them to silence when they shout for blood! This much the world will sure expect of you!

GEN. WASH. — The world is not my judge, loved Martha! I appeal from earth to heaven; from man to God! The world has stoned its prophets, slain its men of pure, white souls; 't will yet excuse Iscariot, and write apologies to bleach his crime to friendship's whiteness! Ay, the world may weep and wring its hands; but we shall not be moved, for we are earnest men, and fight to break our chains, which this base soul would rivet fast with fraud and perfidy! John Andre has polluted freedom's soil, and he must die, for it is holy ground!

MARTHA. — George, George, is there no hope for him?

GEN. WASH. — There's one can save his life Benedict Arnold! Let him come and take his place and Andre's free!

MARTHA. — Beloved, you are so changed! Why do you bend so fierce a look upon your wife! You do not love her now as you were wont in dear Mount Vernon's groves. Oh, hear me, heaven! give our country peace, And me my husband's heart once more.

GEN. WASH. — You wrong me, gentle wife! All that I ever was that am I still to you! Tho' these are times that sorely try men's souls; when women's tears fall hot and fast on new made graves, and all the air is laden with the breath of prayer; yet do my thoughts amid the perils and the noise of war, unbidden turn to our Virginian home where fair Potomac rolls his silver waves! Was it not thus, sweet wife,

(*Resting one knee upon an ottoman.*)

I used to make our statures equal, and was it not thus I used to draw you to my side; and wasn't not thus my heart was wont to speak to yours (*kissing her*), sweet wife, and thus, lest you misunderstood? (*kissing her*.)

MARTHA. — Ay, it was thus (*kissing him*). Forgive me, dearest, noblest, best of men! What would you have me do?

GEN. WASH. — Go rest your weary heart and eyes in sleep.

MARTHA. — I will! Good night.

GEN. WASH. — Good night! Good night!

SENTRY (*outside*). — All is well!

SCENE SIXTH.

GEN. WASH. — He ought to suffer death. No more? Is there no greater judgment for so great a crime? Where lies remorse, where lurks despair? Can we not load them on his soul and let him live for evermore? Is death the hardest blow that man can strike? Then let it fall at once! The swiftness of the shaft shall lend it weight and sink it deeper in his breast! Quick let me sign! Call Hamilton! The sentence is approved! Let execution follow swift and daybreak see the end! Call Hamilton, Good William! William! I am glad he did not hear, for anger must not guide the pen, nor vengeance breathe upon the sad decree! I'll wait till morning comes! I will not sign it now! And yet if it be just, why not. Why not? (*A pause.*) I will not sign it now! William! William! WILLIAM *enters and approaches.*

WM. — Why, heah I was gin'ral! Don ye see me, right heah afo' you?

GEN. WASH. — What's the hour William?

WM. — Purty neah done gone mornin fo' shuah. Gin'ral, de roosters crewed some time ago! I heared dem wid my own ears. Phew, golly molly, jes heah dat wind whistle an' talk in dat chimney Fo' shuah I belieb dere's is spooks in dis ole house, Gin'ral! I hea' all sorts of nizes. I wish I was back in old Virginny, I do" Phew! Dat wind cry jis like a real human pusson! Gin'ral! Gin'ral! Gin'ral!

GEN. WASH. — (*rousing from his reverie*). What is it, my good man?

WM. — Don you dink dose red coats will git sick ob deir job afo' long an clar out ob our kentry, so dat we kin go back to deah ole Mount Wernon an' hab peace an' quiet once more in de family?

GEN. WASH. — God grant it may come soon, soon, soon.

WM. (*aside*). — Poo' Massa Washington, he werry sorrowful to night mus' try to cheer him up a little. (*Loud.*) De odder night, gin'ral, I dreamed I see dose red coats marchin', marchin', marchin' away out ob de laud, an' I fought I heard you say: "Come Willum, my boy, de war is all ober now, no more fightin' wid nobody; let's go home to ole Virginny!" An so we come at last to de ole homestead on de banks ob de ribber, an' I fought I seed you sittin' on de pizarro jus' as you used to sit a long, long time ago, lookin' so pleased and happy, and I fought I heard you say: "Willum, take your banjo and sing me dat ole song I used to lub so to heah;" an' I fought I seed dat brack face of mine all covered ober wid smiles ob joy when I heard you say: "Take de ole banjo an' sing me dat ole song I used to lub so to heah;" and den, I fought I did take dat ole banjo, jis dis way (*takes a banjo out from under the table*), an' den I fought I set down by you, jes dis way, and den I commenced for to sing.

[*Sings a plaintive negro melody.*]

GEN. WASH. — Give me your hand, William!

WM. — Why, Massa Washington, I mean gin'ral, I hab'nt done noffin wrong hab I? Deah Massa Washington, I'm berry sorry I am fo' shuah!

GEN. WASH. — Give it to me I say!

[*William obeys slowly and tremblingly.*]

GEN WASH. — What matters it how black the hand may be if but the heart be pure and good!

WM. (*aside.*) — Heah dat, now, heah dat scoldin' I'm gittin', yes, I deserb it, ebbery word ob it! Massa Washton is berry angry wid me!

GEN. WASH. — Tell me, William, my good man, where were you born?

WM. — Why, Massa Washington, de fust birf —place dat I can perzactly recklemember was way down souf in de Carolinas. I was a berry bad boy an' made de ole folks cry ebbery day. It almost broke my heart to dink of dose days now. I wish I could be born ober again, dear massa. I'd make it all right wid de old folks dis time!

GEN. WASH. — And do you know if they are living still?

WM. — Oh, no, no, no, Massa Washington, dey done gone to de bressed happy land long, long ago! I see deir brack faces lookin' down at me sometimes when I'm done gone asleep, but —but—

GEN. WASH. — Well, speak, what is it?

WM. — But Susie, she ain't dead yet.

GEN. WASH. — Ah, you had a sister then?

WM. — Oh, no, Massa Washington, Susie was my wife, she was de mudder ob my little pickaninny, Zip, jis as libely as a coon an cunnin' as a possum. But one day ole massa eat too much water-melon and so he went feet fust, toes up, and den, an' den —dey took Susie away from me —and dey took little Zip too, fo' dey said 'de little coon would die if dey took him from his mudder, and so dey sold dem boof —an' I never seed dem no more — no more

GEN. WASH. (*springing to his feet*). — Accursed trade! that blights the soul and spreads the leprosy of greed from heart to heart! William! My good and faithful man, I can confide in you! I've proved your heart! Know, then, that by my will, I set my bondmen free upon my wife's decease! But unto you, I give immediate freedom in my will. Old faithful friend of mine, you shall not serve another master! When I'm gone you will be free! May heaven prolong your days in peace and health until the fullest measure has been yours!

WM. — No, no, Massa George, no, no! Don't talk dat way, I don't nebber want no freedom no how! I stay wid you till de angels say: "Hello dar, Willum, it's time to come up, ole man!" an' if you go fast, Massa George, to de bressed happy land, I'll join you dar afo' long. When Massa George is done gone away fo' ebber, den I want to go too den I want to lay dese ole bones down in some quiet corner ob de church-yard—fo' I shant hab no more use fo' dem —an' go lib wid you in de land of de shinin' ribber. I'll be your slave up dar too, Massa Washington—

GEN. WASH. — Silence! (*A pause.*) Call Col. Hamilton.

SENTRY (*outside*). —Twelve is the clock! Twelve is the clock, and all is well!

[*The wind means, the storm increases.*]

GEN. WASH. — Oh, wild, tempestuous night, thy wail shall be his requiem, for now my heart's at peace with God and man.

[A bell strikes, during which Washington paces slowly towards the table.] (Seizing the *pen.*) — I hear and I obey! [*As* WASHINGTON *signs the sentence,*

MRS. ARNOLD *appears at the side with disheveled hair and wild mien.* MARTHA WASHINGTON *enters from opposite side.*]

HAM. (*advancing to the table.*) — When shall the prisoner die?

GEN. WASH. — To-morrow, at sundown!

MRS. A. (*rushing wildly forward.*) — Mercy! mercy! mercy!

SENTRY (*outside*). — All is well!

[*Mrs. Arnold falls senseless. William advances toward her. Curtain on tableau.*]

## END OF ACT FOURTH.

# 1783.

## ACT FIFTH.

**FRANCIS TAVERN NEW YORK.**

SCENE FIRST.

*A Room in the Tavern.*

*Enter Parson* CALDWELL, *in the garb of a country parson, brandishing a cane.* WILLIAM *retreating before him.*

BARON PARSON. — Joshua smote the Amorites, Gideon smote the Midianites, Samson smote the Gazites, David smote the Amalakites and George Washington smote the Albionites, surnamed the "Red Coats," surnamed the "Britishers," that do dwell in an exceeding small island beyond the seas. Yea, verily. Come hither, thou dusky son of Africa. I would speak with the mighty man of valor, the "Great Captain." Why is his chariot so long in coming? Why tarry the wheels of his chariot? Come hither, oh gentle Ethiopian, and impart unto mine ear the whereabouts of the glorious leader, than whom among the children of Israel there is no goodlier person. From the shoulders and upwards he is higher than any of the people. Yea, verily.

WM. — Sah?

PARSON. —Yea, verily, even as King Ahaz called unto Tiglath Pileser, king of Assyria, so the king of England called unto the rulers of the Hessians for help. But the Hessians distressed the King of England and strengthened him not, for verily George Washington smote the Hessians under the fifth rib and despoiled them of their substance. And now, behold, they go down to the sea in their ships, exceeding wroth, and much dissatisfied with themselves and with us. Yea, verily. I would speak with the valiant leader, who hath overcome Gog of the land of Magog, the chief prince of Mesheck and Tubal. Yea, verily!

WM. — Sah?

PARSON. — Yea, verily, I would speak with the mighty man of valor, the chiefest among us, even George Washington.

WM. — Can't do it, sah. De gin'ral receibs no one dis mernin'. Can't do it, sah, I say.

PARSON (*brandishing his cane*). — Bridle thy tongue, oh son of the land of bullrushes, oh mild mannered Ethiopian, lest I wax wroth and smite thee with my staff.

WM. — Take car' dar, sah! Play light, wid dat brack stick, or I'll call de guard. What's de matter wid de man? Take car' dar! Shoo! Go 'way, sah!

PARSON. — Verily, thou dusky son of the land of bullrushes, I'll smite thee if thou dost not announce my coming to the general. Yea, verily, thou deceitful Ethiopian! I am a man of peace, but verily the blood of my veins is waxing warm.

[*Brandishing his stick.*]

WM. (*retreating*). — Take car' dar, man! Put down dat brack stick, or I'll call de guard! Shoo! Go way! I tell you de gin'ral gib no aujience dis morning. Haul in dat brack stick, sah!

PARSON. — Verily, satan hath filled thine heart to lie thou insidious Ethiopian! Thou shalt suffer flagellation! Yea, verily!

[*Pursues him.*]

WM. — Take car dah, man! Stop, stay back, haul in dat brack stick! Shoo! Go way! Don' ye heah! Take car', sah! What you mean, sah! Shoo! Stay back, sah!

## SCENE SECOND.

. —Hey, da! Hey, da! Villiam! Villiam! I will speak mit der Sheneral! (*Entering.*) Ach, mein goot friend der Parson, vat brays mit a sword and breaches mit a musket! Shook hands mit me!

PARSON. — Noble German man! Salutation and greeting! Peace and prosperity abide with thee and thy household, thy servants and thy handmaidens till the end! Yea, verily!

BARON. — Vy, vy, vy! How vos dot peen any vay, you couldn't fix it, hey? You tidn't have get yourself tied to no sword! Your shoulder vos not been got under no musket?

PARSON. — Yea, verily, I have beat my sword into a plough-share and my spear into a pruning-hook! Verily these are the habiliments of peace, most worthy German man! No more shall the red horse of war and he that sitteth thereon take peace from our land, nor shall the people kill one another anymore, for, verily, there is a time to love and a time to hate, a time of war and a time of peace! Yea, verily, most valiant German man!

BARON. — Vell, Barson, I told you now, I vos been ferry glad de var vos come mit her end; shook hands mit me, my olt friend!

PARSON. — Yea, verily, my soul rejoiceth! (*Skipping about.*) Sing, O daughter of Zion! Shout oh Israel! Be glad and rejoice with all thine heart, O daughter of Jerusalem!

BARON. — Ha, ha! Mein freund, I vos peen ferry glat to see you shump for shoy! Pnt, my tear old freund, you tidn't have got no pizness now vat shall you do, hey, to make your putter and bread? Hey, mine pully breacher, told me dat?

PARSON. — Verily, I shall betake myself to the Jerseys, whence I came, and shall administer unto sick and weary souls, even as I did in the olden time, and I shall pursue the peaceful avocation of agriculture; yea, verily, I shall raise ring-streaked, speckled and spotted William goats and brown cattle! Yea, verily, I shall plant red pottage, an abundance thereof, and if thou wilt visit me, most admirable German man, I'll set before the red pottage, well sodden, and a firstling of my flocks and the fat thereof, and thou shalt eat thereof, and drink of the unfermented juice of the apple, and be merry! But no wine or strong drink shall I set before thee, for just as sure as the churning of milk bringeth forth butter, or the wringing of the nose bringeth forth blood, so does the partaking of wine and strong drink end in riot and disturbance! Yea, verily!

BARON. — Vell, I dinks I excepts dat leetle inwitation, mein freund. I dinks I vent over and saw you a leetle in dose Sharseys.

PARSON. — Heartfelt thanks, most excellent German man. Thou shalt be welcome, and abide with me in my humble habitation. Yea, verily, for better is a handful with quietness than both hands full with travail and vexation of spirit. Yea, verily!

BARON. — Yes, mein freund, dat vos peen ferry drue! Better have an empty head osh an empty stomach — hey, pully breacher?

PARSON. — Ha, ha, ha! Yea, verily, thine observations are spiced with much of wit and humor. They tickle my diaphragm, and cause me to burst into exceeding mirth. Ha, ha, ha!

BARON. — Ha, ha, ha! Pully breacher! Dat vos peen right laugh and shump for shoy!

PARSON. — Yea, verily, most lovable German man. I will gambol and be rejoiced, for we have hanged the British lion on an exceeding high and exceeding sour apple-tree, fifty cubits at least, even as high as Ahasuerus hanged Haman!

BARON. — Ha, ha, ha! Mein freund, you vos always been a pully breacher, any vay you couldn't fix it. Ha, ha, ha mein heart was filled mit shoy. I feel as lively as a grasshopper! I could shump as high as a gricket!

PARSON. — Yea, verily, most generous German man, my heart is likewise full of gladness. Even as David danced with all his might, so will I gambol and leap-about in my joy! [*Skips about.*]

BARON. — Ha, ha! Mein freund, der pully breacher, shook hands mit me. Ha, ha, ha! Giss me on de sheek!

PARSON. — Yea, verily, I will greet thee with a kiss of thanksgiving and gladness.

(*They kiss and then dance about.*)

BARON. — Stop a leetle, step a leetle, mein freund. Mein goodness gracious mein pody all come out of my breath! Phew I didn't have got no vind left. Phew! Stop a leetle, I forgot to make my peezness here, I will speak mit our tear Sheneral!

PARSON. — Yea, verily, most amiable German man, with like intent came I hither. Lo! The Ethiopian abideth in the corridor; let us summon him and make inquiry.

BARON (*calling*). — Hey da, Villiam! Hey da! Vere you vos peen all der vile? I vill speak a leetle mit der Sheneral.

PARSON. — Ho, good Ethiopian, faithful servitor, attend, approach, give ear.

[*Enter* WILLIAM.]

BARON. — Villiam, my poy, ve vill speak mit der Sheneral.

PARSON. — Gentle Ethiopian, this most dutiful German man and myself, behold we crave his Excellency's permission to stand before him and pay our homage!

WM. — Sorry, gemmen, but I hab de strictest orders to admit no one. De gin'ral berry much occlepied.

PARSON. — Verily, these words are as bitter to mine ear as the waters of Marah to the lips! Most honored German man, we must depart with sorrowing hearts, and await the pleasure of our beloved Commander. Yea, verily!

BARON. — Yes, mein freund, ve must vent home mit salt water in our eye! Hey, da! Villiam! Villiam!

[*He turns to* WILLLAM *in dumb-show; his sword gets between the parson's legs.*]

PARSON (*embarrassed*). — Verily, the accoutrements of war have become entangled with my peaceful and unoffending limbs! I will sojourn in this abode no longer! The abomination of desolation overtaketh me! Harken unto me, most admirable German man! Verily, he doth converse so intently with the gentle Ethiopian that he heareth me not! (*Very loud.*) Give ear unto my voice, most illustrious German man!

BARON. — Vell, vell, mein friend, vot vos been der matter mit you?

PARSON. — Verily, I will sojourn in this abode no longer, most judicious German man!

BARON. — Vell, vell, mein freind, come, vent home mit me and drink a leetle glass of Rhine vine to our Sheneral's health!

PARSON. — Nay, nay, most hospitable German man, I will partake of no fermented wine nor strong drink, it worketh abomination in my stomach and setteth a flame in my blood; it causeth me to regret that I was ever born, and maketh my tongue to cleave to the roof of my month. When I arise from my couch it visiteth me with remorse and with a thirst that is exceeding difficult to quench, even as the thirst of the rich man who beheld Abraham afar off and Lazarus in his bosom! Nay, most enticing German man, I will betake myself to the land of Jersey, which is beyond the river called Hudson's, and sojourn among my kindred! Yea, verily!

BARON. — Vell, mein freund, shook hands mit me! May you be happy till I saw you again once more! Goot pye, pully breacher. Take me in your bosom and giss me on the sheek.

PARSON. — Yea, verily, I will salute thee with a friendly kiss! Fare thee well, genial German man. Even as Jeshuron waxed fat and kicked, so may you grow thick, and may fatness cover you! Fare thee well; yea, verily, fare thee well!

BARON. — Goot pye goot pye dear, ole pully breacher, Took goot care mit yourself!

[*They pass out.*]

## SCENE THIRD.

*Enter* WASHINGTON, *reading a letter.*

"Our freedom is achieved, but not secured! 'Twas common danger held these colonies so firmly bound together! That is past! To you, illustrious sir, the people turn. You are the idol of the army: speak and you shall be obeyed! A sceptre lies within your grasp, a crown awaits your brow: reach out and seize the royal diadem! The nation will consent, the world applaud! Build up a broad and mighty empire 'neath these western skies and wear its crown! Fear naught, the hour has come! Be quick, be strong, be king!

[*He paces the floor excitedly.*]

I hear the message, but I heed it not! Will royal mantle still my troubled heart when dark remorse has robbed it of its rest? Can jeweled crown give peace to anxious mind that holds remembrance of its wrongful deeds? Be king, say'st thou? I hear thy voice, beloved Mount Vernon, calling loud and clear! Be not afraid. I would not barter' way thy shores and groves, thy brooks and fields, thy peace and love, to wear the brightest crown that ever graced a monarch's brow! Who bids me, then, be king? Be king? ay, true, my country men I would be king, and reign in your affections with unrivaled sway, your hearts my throne your love my crown and your respect the sceptre I would wield! What, cry you still "Be king, be king!" O dream of kingly power and regal state that buildest up so dazzling bright and fair; thy silken cords are chains, thy crown is wound with thorns, thy palaces are prisons, no, no, no, I will not enter in!

[*Tears the letter and throws the pieces into the fire.*] Enter *Officer.*
OFFICER (*Saluting*). — The generals of the American army.
GEN. WASH. — Admit them!
[*A pause.*]

## SCENE FOURTH.

Enter GENERAL GREENE, GENERAL KNOX, MARQUIS DE LA FAYETTE, BARON STEUBEN, COL. HAMILTON *and other officers. They salute* WASHINGTON *respectfully.*

GEN. WASH. —Companions in aims! 'Tis eight long years since Concord's plains first drank of patriot blood, and yet methinks thro' all that time no deeper shadow ever hung about my soul than shrouds it now, for I have summoned you to speak a last farewell. Yes, loyal hearts, whom these long years of hope and fear have knit so close to mine, the end has come at last, and England's monarch speaks us free and independent States! My task is done! From hence I hasten to the halls of Congress; there surrender up the high and sacred trust I've held so long, and crave consent from that august assemblage to become once more a simple citizen! O, would my lips had power to tell the love and gratitude with which I take my leave of you! Come, gather round me once again, my chosen friends, and let me feel the grasp of each one's hand before I go from hence! You, General La Fayette, oh noble name yet nobler heart, whom two worlds love the young republic's friend, my friend, my son, this is the place for you; (*opens his arms*); farewell, farewell!

LA FAY. — Farewell, beloved commander, fare you well.

GEO. WASH. (*to the others*). — Farewell, farewell!

STEUBEN. — Farewell, noblest and best of men!

GREENE. — God bless George Washington!

PARSON. (*rushing forward and grasping Washington by the hand*). — Amen! So mote it be! Yea, verily!

*Tableau.*

## SCENE FIFTH.

A STREET IN NEW YORK.

*Flags, triumphal arches, cheering, music and chimes. The music draws near and passes across the stage; then appear Washington's body-guard, and following them a troop of children and Washington on horseback. The children, clad in pure white, strew flowers in front of the hero and sing:*

"Welcome, mighty chief, once more,
Welcome to this grateful shore,

Now no mercenary foe
Aims again the fatal blow,
Aims at thee the fatal blow!
Virgins fair and matrons grave,
These thy conquering arms did save,
Build for thee triumphal bowers;
Strew, ye fair, his way with flowers,
Strew your hero's way with flowers."

*William walks beside Washington's horse. Hamilton and other aids follow their general Scene withdrawn. Capitol at Washington disclosed. Curtain falls upon the tableau.*

## END OF ACT FIFTH AND OF THE DRAMA.

www.ingramcontent.com/pod-product-compliance
Lightning Source LLC
Chambersburg PA
CBHW020431010526
44118CB00010B/530